Oceans

Bruce Meyer

Toronto

Exile Editions
2004

Copyright © BRUCE MEYER 2004
Copyright © EXILE EDITIONS LIMITED 2004

All rights reserved. The use of any part of this publication, reproduced, transmitted in any form or by any means, electronic, mechanical, photocopying, recording or otherwise stored in a retrieval system, without the prior consent of the publisher is an infringement of the copyright law.

This edition is published by Exile Editions Limited,
20 Dale Avenue, Toronto, Ontario, Canada   M4W 1K4

Sales Distribution:
McArthur & Company
c/o Harper Collins
1995 Markham Road
Toronto, ON
M1B 5M8
toll free:
1 800 387 0117
(fax) 1 800 668 5788

Composition & Design by MICHAEL P.M. CALLAGHAN
Author Photo by JOHN REEVES
Typeset at MOONS OF JUPITER, TORONTO, ONTARIO
Printed and Bound at GAUVIN IMPRIMERIE, HULL, QUEBEC

The publisher wishes to acknowledge the assistance toward publication of the Canada Council and the Ontario Arts Council.

ISBN 1-55096-627-8

For Kerry and Katie who pulled me from the waves

...and the water was so clear that the monks could see every movement of life beneath; so clear, indeed, that the animals on the ocean bed seemed near enough to touch. If the monks looked down into the deep, they could see many different kinds of creatures lying on the sandy bottom like flocks at pasture, so numerous that, lying head to tail, and moving gently with the swell, they looked like a city on the march.

— The Voyage of St. Brendan

I have great comfort from this fellow: methinks he hath no drowning mark upon him; his complexion is perfect gallows. Stand fast, good Fate, to his hanging! Make the rope of his destiny our cable, for our own doth little advantage. If he be not born to be hanged, our case is miserable.

— William Shakespeare
The Tempest, I.i.

Contents

In Sand, To a Daughter Approaching Seven • *1*

The Bay of Bengal • *2*

The Odysseus Limericks • *3*

The Shells • *5*

Bréf Double by Candlelight • *7*

Tempest • *8*

Ties • *10*

The Swimming Pool • *11*

Theology • *13*

The Last Resort • *14*

Grapefruit • *16*

Going to Nantucket • *17*

Parenthood • *19*

Undersea Aquarium, St. Thomas • *20*

Navigatio • *21*

Caribbean Blue • *23*

A Florida Sestina • *24*

Kingfishers from the Subway • *26*

Dripping Wet • *28*

Lifeboat Practice • *29*

Early • *31*

The Lighthouse at Honfleur • *32*

Royal Life-Saving Course • *34*

Blue Heaven • *35*

Penelope's Song • *36*

Katie and the Bouquet of Dandelions • *38*

Inland • *39*

The Order of the Bath • *40*

Cyclops • *41*

Calypso • *42*

Homeric Laughter • *44*

The River Merchant's Boys • *46*

The Rainy Season • *47*

Trompe l'Oeil • *51*

Goldfish • *53*

Baptism • *55*

Parade of Lights • *56*

The Last Northern Poem • *58*

Short-Wave • *59*

Liner Notes • *60*

My Beautiful Father • *62*

Drowning in Books • *63*

Home Port • *65*

Oceans • *66*

Notes • *70*

Acknowledgements • *74*

Biography • *75*

In Sand, To a Daughter Approaching Seven

You wander away when I'm talking to you
because grass and trees and growing things
know that the only real distance between sun
and leaf is the distance of a split second
when the earth moves through enormous space
leaving the past behind.

And when we sat on the beach and castled
our checkerboard with knights and pawns,
building up and tearing down again, you
left footprints on way to the water's edge
and they pointed to a distant shore as if
they could almost reach it.

A handful of sand scattered on the wind,
a blessing of spirit moving upon the earth,
fingers once held you no longer need,
an empty branch in winter reaching out—
oh, if I had touch to make the springtime come
closer I'd pull the sun.

I whisper in your ear each night a prayer
like the angel asking Caedmon to sing—
a word of beginning but never farewell,
you wander away but you can still hear me
because grass and trees, all growing things
desire to become themselves.

The Bay of Bengal

It is not a question of what you dream
but how far you can will your vision.
Believe in the ability to make everything seem

not what it is but what it might redeem.
Here a beach on Lake Huron; here its elision.
It is not a question of what you dream.

Let the sand, sun and each sparkling beam
sunlit on wave choir into an expression
of desire. Running to madness the truth may seem

a continent away, so far away a moonbeam
shining on a temple leaves the impression
of eternity. Desire's what you think you dream.

A god opens his eye, loosing a natal scream.
His voice crescendos to a *Kyrie eleison*
and love is born to make everything seem

all everything can be, love that can transform
the meaning of a summer day's expression
into a grain of sand, the beautiful and supreme
vision that brushed by you in a dying dream.

The Odysseus Limericks

I counted the endless waves
as songs released from staves.
The notes that were drowned
were the last siren sound
of a mind that constantly raves.

I dreamt my sailors were living,
pulling on oars and still thriving,
and in each watered eye
they implored the stark sky
for mercy the gods are not giving.

Having journeyed and found but desire
I longed for my hearth's dying fire.
Though I take to the grave
all the world I can't save,
the truth will make me a liar.

So I went ashore to find peace
but the sea wouldn't give me release;
each night as I woke
the moon and tide spoke
your wanderings never shall cease.

I'll shoulder my winnowing fan
declare I'm a lucky man,
find a grove or a garden
where I'll seek the sea's pardon
make amends and begin again.

MEYER

There once was a man from an island
a lover of cities, a brigand.
When life slaughtered hope
he found he could cope.
He survived, but he can't understand.

The Shells

Mornings after fierce storms when the sea
was smooth as ice and melting before our eyes,
my mother, grandfather and I would be
in shorts, on the beach, wading to our thighs
through shallows, the white light of heavenly
non-complicity reflected in our faces to reprise
a rainbow innocence among shards and debris.

It was the rare time we saw each other's legs—
my grandfather's thin and worn from a century
of having stood against the violent dregs
of change, my mother's beautiful and girlishly
white, and mine like fragile saplings, little twigs
driven into the sand, absurd as a gull's spindly
pylons— and for what we found we gave thanks.

Jingle shells, moon snails, quahogs and clams,
dwarf welks and angel wings, widow's purses
and sand collars—we'd be clothed in shams
of riches, stuffed pockets full, gently nurse
the most delicate finds, arrange them in lines
on the kitchen table to await their next curse,
a new death, living under assumed names.

Instead of the voice of the sea within them
they would live by the stories we would tell,
how jingle shells were coins struck for Neptune,
how angels shed outgrown wings that fell
to earth like snowflakes. A smooth pink moon
shell in our hands was equally celestial,
driving tides toward the inevitable *too soon*.

And when they had no stories left to offer,
when dust settled on them and grew tired
of the same thing, seasons, the endless winter...
when our footprints became shards and melted
into the farthest place from live sea air
leaving not a wrack behind, our voices expired,
oceans persisted without us, imagining who we were.

The beauty of stories is the beauty of change;
tide lines strewn with treasured remains
after a night of flux and rearrangement;
the life still found in death that explains
why I listen to a shell for its strange
ruminations, echoes of tides, the pains
of passage, time's novel estrangement.

The story of every shell peering from the jar—
all that remains of a shelling expedition
forty summers ago—speaks like an old scar
whispering to a lover from smooth skin,
saying simply *I am alright now, I've come far,
I've put it all behind me.* Let the stories begin.
An angel wing, once in heaven, brushed a star...

Bréf Double by Candlelight

The power is out all over the country.
Cricket song ends the day with blind love.
Tune in to the constant cottage clock.
Mars is risen, sun-burnt in the east.

Sit with me in the brief glow of candlelight.
What if ancient spirits feel the sudden shock,
the absence of our driven light and energy—
what if they loved what we did best?

We hurt our eyes, sitting here, reading
as if Milton in some other century:
darkness overtook him. A ripe moon
makes a better lamp. It will rise and feast
on soft ripples in the bay as fry
feed on shadows beneath the dock.

Tempest

Read Shakespeare. In all his drumming
iambics, I hear a heart beating in each
hammered phrase, turned with the glow
of diamonds upon the sadness of dread
and Elizabethan melancholy. His wife
somewhere in the provinces, his last child
crying *Where's Daddy?* his words shopped
to groundlings. Speaking for the commons,
it was just a matter of putting to the test
all life taught him. Pain is a sturdy crutch.

I sing a fool's song not worth humming,
rasped until I outstretched my reach.
And when I pause mid-career now
to take account, I wonder if the dead
had stones in their shoes: pebbles are rife.
They must be pearls. The trusting child
in me wanted to love the world. I dropped
on my knees offering a silent summons
to joy each night, but time does not rest.
Every dream ended with a startling touch.

Is it any easier when you see it coming?
A wall of wind and water at the beach,
or a grey-yellow beard of highway snow
that opens its arms on the road ahead?
I was told: never pray for an easy life.
I swam in the sea as the sky grew wild,
pressed on when I should have stopped—
agonized, wondering if I'm a good person,
feeling not at home but a perpetual guest
wanting more from life but not getting much.

OCEANS

O tempest for a teapot, boil drumming
on steel kettle's skin, the attempted speech
of water undergoing change, the slow
circling of steam paving the way for bread
and wine, tell me if it all comes down to life,
tea and sympathy on an afternoon defiled
by memories: the beloved who eloped
on someone else's ladder, or the come-ons
of last year's hopes, as each passing tempest
waters the lawn, tops the pool, and such.

Ties

My grandfather's ties were navy cockades
trimming the necklines of serge three-pieces.
He wore a fresh one everyday for decades.

My father's foreign-hands were grey. Creases
from travelling appeared below his knot
but blended with his stripes in a road map
of obscure mid-west destinations caught
in amber waves, the labyrinthine trap.

A neck's cold without that fret of hand
folded over and under, tied each morning
in a fealty of pure silk, a Gordian grand
illusion of control, a tongue thirsting to sing.

I will loosen it now, let down my guard,
reprieved from swinging in the prison yard.

The Swimming Pool

The deep end is the happy home
of silence, concrete and shining chrome.

A wad of hair clings to the drain
begging mermaids for song again

as a band-aid of pink wormy bait
slipped its hook for a better fate.

The august sun forms sharp mosaics
reshaping glare with choked prosaics

while on the bottom where light scatters
perception turns to other matters.

The weightlessness of outer space,
the inner chill of sleep's embrace—

one simple, so familiar breath
could change refreshment into death

while monitors of helplessness
cannot tell that there's distress.

What's left behind, that place above
is seldom safe for life or love.

Who says, who dares hope can float?
Are words still burning in a throat

MEYER

that harmonized with siren songs,
and sucked their secrets into lungs?

Look up. Behold the wavering sun.
The enchanted drifting has begun.

Theology

Desiring at three a.m. to enter it,
uncertain if the vestibule's still lit
I fumble on the threshold for a key.
Sleeper, sleep on and dream of me.

The Last Resort

I am weary with this solitude
as a eunuch on his wedding night.
Through trees upright in rectitude
the sadness of a pool's retort,
a lake shimmering beneath the pain
of jet skis whirring in refrain
like mosquitoes hungry for a bite;
O spirit save me from the last resort.

We came, saw, sought sane replies
to stress that drove us all up north,
and choked with chambermaids of flies
took vacuumed rooms facing a port
where moored white launches rest
and rich men strut their gangled best
having summoned courage and gone forth
unto the bar at the last resort.

I shall grow weary, even mad.
The body rests but not the mind.
Perhaps it wouldn't be so bad
if nature's heart was a mighty fort,
and the purity of kitchen smoke
was soul's release the spirit spoke.
The tortured world reborn in kind
has checked in to the last resort.

We'll share a bath, perhaps a bed,
love and long, write postcards home;
say the rest has done us good,
fond regards with a fine report.
They'll find our souls nailed to a tree,
crucified for kings to see—
the sanctity of kingdom come,
sings the beauty of the last resort.

Grapefruit

To my father, it was an expression
of devotion, standing by the sink
each Sunday morning, a surgeon
operating on a heart. Now with ink

in my blood, the pen my blade,
I strive for precision in what I say,
carefully cutting sections made
by nature in the best possible way

to sit on your tongue. This is how I
give you our full and bitter sweet
love, the squirt that stings the eye:
how much life can your soul eat?

Circumnavigating the equator, I run
the cut pressing deeper and deeper
to the source. Light pours from the sun
as I drive my knife to the heart's core.

Going to Nantucket

A half-mile off Hyannis with the wind
blowing in our faces just to be unkind,

one by one, you threw the seashells back,
I accounting lines from a prayer book,

to make certain death would be death,
saving the last word, *Amen*, for the truth.

Time to cut our losses, you would say,
time to cut into shifting sands as sea

depreciates the flesh of continents, grains
once solid mountains clinging to the remains

of their origins, life that refuses to die
even when faced with oblivion or eternity,

a cheque written on water for an indelible
instant, the proximity of the improbable.

Collect what is owed you. Collect yourself
as if you were stooping in white surf

to catch a jingle shell, a rare florin
crested before tumbling away again,

crowned with the draffiness that lost
and fading things use to tempt us, the last

good words we had together that day
as the morning sky grew red and the sea

rose up to meet it, pouring all over us.
Running for the Atlantic Café, the rush

of cold eating its way through bones,
our silly sacrifice was not enough. Dunes,

fields, mountains, even the stars above
should have been thrown back to prove

there was more to us than dull ritual.
Dripping in the café to the disapproval

of the barman who served up coffee,
though spirits were what he thought we

needed, we waited out the sea,
certain of the resurrection of the body,

committed to the deep drowned world,
investing its existence in a mere word.

Let's assume things *can* last forever:
love, hope, beauty (valuables braver

than anything in time's lousy catalogue)
deposited in that guarded bank of fog

just beyond where the storm is drawn
revealing a surprise behind the curtain.

Parenthood

At dawn we sited a new world,
but stars we'd steered by foundered.

At times adrift, map still in hand,
we hold on tight and sing.

Undersea Aquarium, St. Thomas

The day I finally put the ring on your finger
we took a practice plunge beneath the waves,
and hand-in-hand beyond the tourist strand,
strolled glass tunnels through aquamarine.

A diver summoned a choir of angelfish.
A sea turtle, curious as a park pigeon,
hovered nearby and appraised our souls.
Do we make a good couple? Will we pass?

Off he flew into the green-blue depths,
clocking more miles on his ancient odometer.
So what could he tell us having bucked the seas,
what records of happiness, storms and shores

could be read in us if our faces were palms,
the world before us drawn and charted,
the moonlight of his birth a beacon still,
a trail of angelfish harping on stars?

They float so gracefully among the crumbs,
snapping at life, darting and hungry,
yet wary, nervous, their saint eyes widening
salty with tears: pray they'll intercede for us.

Navigatio

Away from the flesh-fry on the afterdeck
we sought a new place to be alone,
you with headphones jogged your laps
sailing in circles like an ancient saint.

My feet found a quiet deck chair,
canopy shaded on the promenade,
and taking out my notebook and pen
felt impelled to claim the expanse.

Amethyst horizon with nothing to say,
blue and empty as a Buddha's bliss,
a quick scan for pegasian flying fish,
seabirds, falling boys, any sign of life:

finding none only drove me on.
The empty page is a kind of thirst.
Scurvy of Magellan, madness of Drake.
Come and get me when I'm finished.

Why was it explorers wrote so much
when far at sea with nothing to do,
life living elsewhere on fecund islands—
the sea a study, a room of one's own.

I'll tell you stories of the wild unknown,
of Utopian islands and great fanged beasts,
of columns of glass and inlets of charm—
it is only a dream afloat on a wish.

MEYER

Will convince myself I found the passage,
direct lines to that prized spice land
where souls have wings and sing in trees,
admonishing it is time to move on.

All I ask is to traverse the unknown,
a sea of blue from my compass point,
a sturdy craft, a star to steer by,
and wind enough to return to you.

Caribbean Blue

The colour of the sky before dusk
when you are far beyond the city lights;

the colour of ink when it describes
a sea so alive words drown in it—

the sadness you taste when a drop of spray
tells you that blue is the colour of sorrow,

the colour of a dream that woke you
when dead friends were suddenly alive;

the colour of mornings when empty sky
waits for the sun to follow you home

so full of life and light and darkness
it is an amethyst, an oracle stone,

a horizon line where you signed your name,
an impossible promise you're bound to keep.

A Florida Sestina

for David Caplan

Last night I dreamt I chased the dolphins.
They passed my open window, a vision
that might have inspired believers to believe
in light, resurrection and everlasting life.
They could not break faith with nature,
the sufferer of all injustice and time.

I walked on the beach and witnessed time.
Far out on the distilled horizon, dolphins
played; the mind was almost ready to say nature
is perfect, but sharp and underfoot a vision:
the crunch of shell shards turning to sand. Life
tempts me with such wonders as I might believe,

for what is the mind but a dream we believe,
the passage of waves that measure time
on a Florida shore, the long beauty of brief life.
I wrote my name in the sand. The dolphins,
silent in their secrets, kept count, another vision
green, eager, sniffing out the temporal nature

that lurks in all things. The mystery nature
would love to have me embrace and believe
with the passion of a creed, was a vision
ecstatic, fluidly supernal and beyond time.
Who could put it into words? Truth is, dolphins
are smarter than humans. They measure life

by the run of current, by the worriless flow of life
in its imperfect wonder, by the threats nature
utters against itself, its neurotic verge. Dolphins
know better because they refuse to believe
in anything but dolphins, that moment where time
is but an instant, the paradise of divine vision

that sees reason in blood's warmth, the vision
of seas as pitiless as yesterdays, the extant life
that began with home, eaten whole by time.
It lived in every broken shell. Comfort me, nature.
Tell me that all the paradises I want to believe
in are just distractions, that I may, like a dolphin,

sing praises to the bright vision of nature
where life is not merely to live but to believe,
as time would have it, blessing the dolphin.

Kingfishers from the Subway

I'd never forget you, I explain,
arriving late at the daycare door.
Even through a senile fog
I'd know you were mine—
you have my eyes, my soul looking back,
my questions too, nesting for answers.

Picking up shards of old brick
on a long hike through the valley,
I stopped and asked what you saw—
two birds, tufted plumes, white bellies,
a sudden splash in the green river,
a hasty exit to a high, bare perch.

Looking from the subway viaduct
as we rattle home pressed to the door—
There they are! I say, and you scan
the valley before a tunnel blacks us.
Don't be disappointed. They're hard to see.
Serendipity isn't just for kingfishers.

Look at the way you saw light today,
long before I opened my eyes.
You didn't fear the day ahead,
just the sense that being here and now
is happiness alive if unnameable.
Its wings flutter in the corner of your eye.

OCEANS

You lift your head from a colouring book
as I arrive at the daycare door.
Let's look for kingfishers on the way,
and I tell you the sad story from myth:
a lovely queen, her handsome king,
the day love taught them how to see.

Dripping Wet

Tide tumbles you from the water,
draping a gauze of diamond
as you find land legs in a totter
of rushing surf. I can only respond
that you are a goddess in kind,
wrapped in towel, my serendipitous find.

A trail of footprints in the sand, this give-
and-take has me taken with your skin.
A sprig of seaweed on flesh could live
for eternity as a symbol of how to begin
to begin again, reborn from choral surf,
singing encouragements to a new earth.

Thus we stand, on the edge of things,
spectators of a sport that wraps the earth,
awed that we could touch the witherings
of something as large as this. Think rebirth,
sex, the longing in me wanting you,
horizon of blue becoming a deeper blue.

We hug but feel the tug of death,
your flesh clammy against my flesh.
And in that moment as we catch our breath
I look at you; our souls almost mesh
though water and body stand between
us and we must wipe each other clean.

Lifeboat Practice

The words to "Nearer My God to Thee"
we should have learned while still ashore.
Before us lies the wine-dark-sea.
We're better off not knowing what's in store.

Stare at the ever-retreating horizon.
Small boats are for heroism or much more.
Shelley in a squall had no life vest on.
We're better off not knowing what's in store.

Think of James Bond, not the *Titanic*,
the *Raft of the Medusa* where arms implore
a faint hope to remedy the panic.
We're better off not knowing what's in store.

Life is a voyage, a voyage to discover
whether you can stand me, whether I'm a bore.
Shipwrecked on an island, can I be your lover?
We're better off not knowing what's in store.

Do we start a republic? Found a Promised Land?
Enslave scaly creatures or show them the door?
Shall we divvy the spoils or keep them at hand?
We're better off not knowing what's in store.

Will the island fly? Will there be cannibals?
How about a blue lagoon we can't ignore?
Let's get naked and cavort with animals.
We're better off not knowing what's in store.

MEYER

Admirable Creighton or Robinson Crusoe,
claim it for God and Spain, then let's explore.
Hand-in-hand on the edge of the sand we go.
We're better off not knowing what's in store.

Early

I left too soon after our loving was done.
Standing by the pay phone, wanting to call,
I was overcome by the intensely beautiful
salutation of your image in the dawn.

The Lighthouse at Honfleur

"Georges," they said, "blue is a sad colour."
It is the colour of a woman's eyes
lifted above the shining streets,
Pigalle, after April rain.
Blue descends on my life
like the silence of a square at dawn;
it walks beyond the market shadows
to ape their subtle casting
and is the first of all colours to fade.

Yesterday the sands were bursting with pink flesh,
rivulet tides of vanishing white
clung to the ankles of children in green
as a woman shook her morning sheets
out the window of the grand hotel.
I have never been able to paint from the past.

I came because I felt the need
to reconstruct the sadness in my life—
because of all the mornings of despair
there may have been a time when I was happy.
Things prove themselves wholly by accumulation.

I may have been a lover
and flung the very edges of the city
beyond the grasp of promises and lies.
But love was never a fiction of mine
and therefore subject to fail.
Last night I listened to the waves.

"But Georges, there are no people there."
"And none in portraiture as well," I said.
Nothing that I ask for can be true—
I asked for vision and was given paint,
for assurance and received a brush.
Even walking by the sea at dawn
I could not fix the exact sensation
of sand grains in my shoe.

The beach settled in a canvas
of feelings that I could not chain.
I was confronted by what I had not done.

And then there was that skiff with darkened sails
and the fiction of its helmsman
heading out toward the sea,
who through the textures of a foreign mind
might, point by exacting point, realize
the ice-blue calm of a single man
who stood watching from the empty strand
as if the loneliest beneath blue sky.

Royal Life-Saving Course

His mask had flown off in the surf
as sharpened green embedded itself

in eyes not even tears could sting.
Who says waves are choruses that sing

of truth when everything seems lost?
Which way is up when up gets tossed?

In gasping awe they hauled him in.
Sand turned sandpaper on his skin,

sea-cold, clammy as sudden death,
calamity stole away his breath.

Breath is the presence of what's divine;
breath is the nerve within the spine;

and pulling on his crucified arms
to break the spell of tragic charms,

they pushed on him to break the cage
that held the waters rapt with rage

until choked, beaten and brought low,
he awoke to cheers and took his bow.

Blue Heaven

The summer I realized I was no longer a child
I lay awake as the waves whispered *Put it away*,
and an offshore breeze made the sharp surf wild.

Still feeling the burn of light upon my exiled
skin, still hunting the hapless freedom of play,
the summer I realized I was no longer a child.

My father became a master, a shadow reviled
because I could look him squarely in the eye,
as an offshore breeze made the sharp surf wild.

I dreamed of becoming an island, a figure styled
on pantomimes of teenage display.
Someone had to notice I was no longer a child.

A cottage window open to the night, the mild
softness of damp air touching me in foreplay
as an offshore breeze made the sharp surf wild—

what was manhood, what was truth? The child
cut and arranged, blue hydrangea, the worldly way.
More than a summer died. I was no longer a child.
In the neap of my body, the sharp surf ran wild.

Penelope's Song

Unteach them, Muses. Tell the truth,
and if that fails then lie to them
with all the beauty of my youth
I threw away for love on him.

When he sailed away I was young.
My little boy ran me haggard.
The house got beyond me. I wrung
my hands with despair, tired

of watching the horizon each day,
imagining him with his friends
drunk on gore and butchery,
fools striving toward their ends.

Something had to be done. The land
went riotous with weeds. Vagabonds
sat in the courts. Every brigand
declared himself king. Wounds

run deeper when they're self-inflicted,
so I took command. From the few good
left to me I appointed counsellors, indicted
the rabble, and brought peace and food

to Ithaca, running the nation as it had
never been run, creating a beautiful no-place
from desires I had always carried.
There no other country could keep pace

where men and women were equal,
where a week's hard work meant three
of rest and learning. As monarch of all
my people I loved them with a delicacy

that interwove life with love and beauty.
I spent my days at the loom, creating
tapestries announcing our new history.
Then he returned, years on, dissipating

all I had done. He murdered my counsellors,
tore up irrigation systems, taxed
the tenantry and drove the varied vendors
into the blood red sea. Afraid, I asked

him why he would treat his people so,
why he would put his story, odd as it was,
before the truth. Kings come and go,
he said, but he, saved from the jaws

of death would proclaim his story.
He blinded the poet then told him what to write.
But I remain at my weaving, my glory.
One loose thread can lead to daylight.

Katie and the Bouquet of Dandelions

I frame this moment for a winter night
when the wind is ceaseless and I need your light,

when there seems no end or place to begin,
let me picture the butter-glow under your chin.

Inland

They would go down in the earth,
navigating a sea of radioactive stone,
surfacing to winter nights or days
hot enough to melt light from the sky.

Navigating a sea of radioactive stone
they thought of energy in their darkness,
hot enough to melt light from the sky.
They wore blue coveralls and yellow hard hats.

They thought of energy in their darkness,
the spirit energy that opposes igneous shield;
they wore blue coveralls and yellow hard hats
and their diamond drills down to dull bits:

the spirit energy that opposes igneous shield.
They would wear themselves to their dignity
and their diamond drills down to dull bits.
The site was exhausted before they were.

They would wear themselves to their dignity,
then home to a prefab house on a winding street—
the site was exhausted before they were—
stare into an auroraed sky. A boy crosses a field,

then home to a prefab house on a winding street,
pauses because a glow emanating from a window
stares into an auroraed sky. A boy crosses a field,
picks up a stone and hurls it against the night.

The Order of the Bath

Between Scylla and Charybdis of my thighs
floats a pinkened mariner longing for home,

and each lapping wave, each legward breeze
is a sign of love past and love still to come.

A sketchy mind draws this bath, a womb
refuge above body temperature, an old story,

fascination of glittering skin, Renoir's dame
rising from a soak, transformed in the glory

of naked admiration. When I fall in love
with such inner peace my body strives to find,

this chrome-faucetted tub fits like a glove,
a vessel bearing me to Blessed Isles, the kind

warmth that means the world in the dying day,
welcome shores recalling I was born this way.

Cyclops

Magic has only one eye and it stares
over the imaginative sea waiting
for a sheep-white sail caught unawares
by the lilt of song-waves singing.

Magic closes its one eye, becomes a dream
that has no exits, the bed still unmade
and smelling of its shape, the scream
waking itself at night, the dreadful shade

come to claim its niche in adamant—
magic longs to dance but finds itself alone,
criticism that stings from salt, the scant
love that hurls a heartbroken stone

at passersby, the child whose cranium
fused into a petrified monovision asking
if the sun would still love it when warm
blood left its body and paired eyes basking

in their tedious arrogance questioned how
nature could have been so blind or wine
so sweet to make magic drowsy. Go now.
Visiting hours are over. This is magic's time.

Calypso

i)

If only by desire I would dance with you
in the deep of passion, outlast the star dark fire
dying in the chaos beneath Aurora's urgent blue—
if only by desire.

Your kiss is continents. Your softness could inspire
centuries. Could make me abandon my true
self. We could live on lust and never tire.

But your breath on my cheek tells me who
I am— not the immortal hero you admire
but a man called home to be what he must do…
if only by desire.

ii)

Let's live on desire. We will dance to calypso
rhythms while little mai tais slowly perspire
on our table. Tonight you have a goddess glow.
Let's live on desire

because little flames of bamboo torches can fire
that sparkle of starlight in your eyes as the lanai
opens seaward to its steady basso choir

of enchanted melodies. I'll pretend you
are my island mistress as we dance and conspire
to burn our tickets home. You did? Me too.
Let's live on desire.

iii)

If I had enough money I'd quit this dull island.
The days are long, the sky too damn sunny.
I'd float away, bag and belongings in hand
if I had enough money.

He thought it was him. He looked so funny
standing there pleading, *You don't understand,
I'm a king. I've got to be somewhere. Honey,*

I said to him, *Put away the head. The gland
is a much better judge.* But one night his gunny
was gone. I was alone again on the strand.
It's not about the money.

Homeric Laughter

La forza del destino, accidents happen,
the tides washing the shore, *I am, I am*.
When Jacopo Peri invented opera,
gathering his friends in the Camerata,

he may have been influenced by a poet,
Vincenzo Galilei, who dreamt of stars
while drafting a son; and nonetheless,
it moves. The search for opera was the search

for music in the in the soundless cry
of life and life's aftermath, O agape
at the core of tragedy, hewn young Greeks
marching forward in boyish beauty.

Who sings for the countless mornings
when we rise and dress, kiss and part,
or of the evenings when there's not enough day
and out of pity we close our eyes?

Think of the persistence of rain,
how it iambs against the skylight
to the metre of a steadfast heart.
Is this the sound of persistent life?

Think of the sad irony of an army
pyrrhic to its death and dancing
out the rhythm of an anxious heart
in the small hours of a love-torn night—

or the sound of our child's life
struggling to begin on monitored screen,
a blip of yellow bouncing forward...
if you know the words then sing along.

Life, after all, is a beautiful opera,
full of passion, pity, joy and regret,
but worth reloading the charger again,
voices for the house on grey mornings—

When the opera is over and the curtain's
down like eyelids on a Hindu god
creating and destroy all he sees,
I will walk you back in the soft spring rain,

holding your hand, sensing your pulse,
the steady rhythm of waves within us,
salt enough to sting, deep enough to drown,
smitten with the beat that brings us home.

The River-Merchant's Boys

While my hair was cut straight across my forehead
I played about the front gate, pulling flowers,
until, chased away by the old woman's broom
I ran for my Schwinn, and she cursed me dead.
A little bit of china on the lawn, a broken gnome—
while my hair was cut straight across my forehead
like Moe, the angry Stooge. My soul set to harden
in a mask of rage—mean little bugger—sitting for hours
tossing rocks in a stream. Returning to her garden,
I played about the front gate, pulling flowers.

You came by on bamboo stilts, playing horse,
you walked about my seat, playing with blue plums.
Pinkish cherry petals descended in soft showers.
Gonna get her? you asked, and I replied, *Of course.*
She'll hand over the kite even if it takes several hours.
You came by on bamboo stilts, playing horse—
and maybe we could peer in her window and see
what the old witch is doing. Suddenly, out she comes.
She swung. Hit you in the nuts. Missed me.
You walked about my seat, playing with blue plums.

And we went on living in the village of Chokan:
two small people, without dislike or suspicion.
You took over our father's liquor store, became
a notary public on the side while I languished, began
my long slide into propriety. Everyone knows my name.
And we went on living in the village of Chokan:
damned if we did, bored if we didn't. They had it
coming. Such beautiful little targets for destruction.
Tonight let's get hammered and leave something shattered;
two small people, without dislike or suspicion.

The Rainy Season

Summer should be the time of year
      when everything is in sharp focus,

as if someone dropped a quarter
      in panoramic binoculars and you'd

swear you can see the towel you left to dry
      on the chair by your hotel room window

half the city away from the Eiffel Tower.
      Such clarity, you remark, is memorable,

as beautiful as postcards sold by the old man
      on the quayside steps to the Bateau Mouche.

But it has rained for six days straight,
      and not a word of sunlight has passed

from the lips of dour fruit-stand vendors
      who don't understand your sign for melon.

And just when you think of Parisian sewers
      overflowing with tears from Sacre Coeur,

and the odd Jean Valjean bubbling up
      through an antique grating beneath your feet,

you awaken to the screened-in porch,
      the lake face pock-marked like an eager teen,

a travel magazine gone damp in your hands,
      the illusion of beauty called for rain.

The lake level looks higher than in years,
        and questions nag: will the cottage float?

Should the dog be called in? Are the animals paired?
        Suspicions of the flood are pure old-hat,

blustering fears from childhood Noahs,
        the bearded god-toy who stood by the ark,

Deucalion from story books, a bag of stones.
        The Aztecs believed the world would drown,

would die by water in the four destructions;
        to hedge their bets they built floating gardens,

a better world made from pottery shards,
        lush and fluent as a musical phrase,

the song etched in a record of red clay,
        the artist behind all things still singing.

This month is August, named for an emperor,
        named for greatness, a year's eighth month,

the traveller's time, the season of wanderings
        and dog-starred vacations claimed for the courage

of flagging and conquering, greenery at apex,
        life's farthest reach, fecund love in middle age,

the cry of desire welling deep within, the night familiar
        because passion needs comfort. Passion needs focus.

OCEANS

If anything's worth keeping from this humid slumber
    of days where we dreamed while iron rain fell,

drops at snare practice on the sheet-metal roof,
    cooling like beds, love half-made;

a thought that wakes you in the breathless night,
    tells you now the rain has vanished;

a moon-filled sky, its stars and myth dots,
    arms round a world crying itself sane,

that got up, washed its face and looked in a mirror
    to ask itself to believe again, to see its way clear

to places once dreamed of but never achieved,
    the focus of eyes adjusting to starlight.

Let us go there, we belong in our visions.
    Look outward across a city of lights,

a sea of stars above pigeoned streets,
    reflections of tour boats sailing dark rivers,

the tourists with cameras traversing the labyrinth,
    inquiring ways from strangers and dreamers,

longing to rent the temple's grey veil,
    the mourning cloak worn with stoic dignity,

the mark of those who have something to lose,
    something as simple as the slate grey sky

that settles for less because it fears its own grief,
    the quarter that drops when the vision is over,

the startling reality of life looking back,
    the eyes of a god that open and close,

the moon through clouds as weather changes,
    that moment you think you can see forever.

Trompe l'Oeil

I turned off the living room lamps
after the guests had gone home;
someone had forgotten his shadow.

Shadow held out his empty goblet.
Asked for more wine. Just sat there.
An illusion waiting to be entertained.

I had not invited speculation,
nonetheless he made himself at home.
We sat in awkward silence for an hour.

What do you say to a shadow? *Do you enjoy jokes?*
hoping to break the deadlocked calm.
I noticed the trees in my old painting

were rustling to a sympathetic wind,
the light changing as clouds blew by.
Time passed as in Monet's cathedrals.

I remembered the door at Chatsworth,
a violin done-up, waiting to be crushed,
the sad music of an inconsolable soul

wafting through the night like crying,
the beloved a mere street away,
a circling taxi, searching for home.

Let's wait for the doorbell to ring,
welcome whatever comes along.
Maybe it's real and of our making.

Maybe daylight on unsteady legs,
a guest who couldn't sleep without it ,
the truth of myself I'd hate to forget.

Goldfish

I find myself in the uncomfortable seat
of my old high-school auditorium,
and I wait for my number to come up.
It's stifling in this recital of strangers.
And suddenly, the new school arrives—

fluttering in their gold and yellow lamé,
finning with fans in a circular motion,
as if soaring on wings through endless sky.
My daughter's a goldfish. Oceans teem.
I am swept in the ballet of the swim,

flowing as if the sea was light,
a vision treading on tip-toes at night,
the delicacy of articulate fin-like hands
wrapping themselves around my fingers,
facing life's current with wide staring eyes.

Katie dances her way into civilization,
washed and watched over by aeons of song,
safety in numbers stepped into measure,
announcing to all leviathans of deep
the sea will not blacken or be vanquished of life.

Poetry can't die so long live goldfish.
It has been absorbed into simpler things,
so that once in a while in the middle of life
the sea will resound like rapt applause,
and infant starlight in children's eyes.

Who would say great themes have left us,
that love, courage, hope and gentleness
have vanished with the dust of wise men
in a century too brutish to retrace its steps?
Smiling, she curtsies, and my pulse dances.

Baptism

The sound of rain falling on a spring night
is the sound of God answering the prayers

of a newly planted garden in a dry land;
the resonance of a thousand children clapping

after the dancers have come to ease,
the voice of leaves reaching up to sky,

the echo of blessings as the seas part,
the rattle of pebbles in the tide's release,

the memory of nights a millennium ago
when divinity explained itself in sand,

when wonder was thirst in a starry sky
waiting to be quenched in a green shoot.

The empty bucket you left outside
will be a small, wild ocean by morning,

and the rising sun will look inside
to reflect on the beauty of its own light.

Parade of Lights

As if out of darkness the stars came down,
ducking under a bridge in the shape of a palm;
on the darkest night of the year
the boats brought light.

What is holiness in the hands of Florida?
The search for Christ among coconut fronds
led three early birds here in shorts;
was it birth or death?

In the beginning God created the world
and set about the task of making light;
tonight the parade of ships
brings word of life.

Santa Claus with neon blue flamingoes
held up by a cross decked in turquoise holly;
its twin in the coastal waterway
struggling to take shape;

this is a time of rebirth, of souls called back,
of lives lived and reinvented, of lengthening days;
this is a time when love arrives
on the wings of snowbirds.

If the sky seems familiar it is because our hopes
flew south to meet us on the chilled sandscape,
and the waves as ever constant
as our breath bear with us.

OCEANS

I want to become a changed man. I want to rise
each morning bathed in the ecstacy of a hope
that belongs to those who believe
God separated the waters

calling us forth from the depths of expectations,
setting afloat a squadron of wild celebrations
to electrify expensive pleasure cruisers
because someone was born.

I saw three ships in the night like constellations
dredged from the sea where the orange sun set,
thrilled to the passion of strung light.
The glow soon left us,

but having seen their arrival, having waited
in the dark for so long to catch a glimpse
of hope from a restaurant parking lot
something died so we can live.

The Last Northern Poem

They all begin with pines bent
in the north wind, almost strangers
in foreign landscape who've spent
their lives seeking a supreme love,
meeting only realities and dangers
and an empty heaven above.

There is always water smooth
as glass and when the sky falls
it turns iron grey as God's truth—
someone wants to speak but can't,
and a cold, austere silence falls
as if a prayer or broken chant.

I am waiting for someone to write
about a kitchen table, Scrabble game
and a bottle of rye, a long night
when yellow glare from the window
shouts at darkness with the glee
of pissing off the porch into snow,
with steam rising clear enough to see.

And for that moment when dawn
is not a flight of geese in chevron
but a love-worn cottage yawn
as stale as old books we read,
knowing the stories would remain
to haunt us as we haunt the dead.
We kiss. The window beads with rain.

Short-Wave

Flying through nowhere on an afterdeck
of the Norwegian liner, a tropical cumulus

rising around pale outlines of Bahamas
or some other nameless destination dark

as the mysteries of undiscovered lands,
you tuned the short-wave in your hands

and the world sang. Propaganda, praise,
song from languages flowing like stars

beyond the vast edges of starlit galaxies,
our ears absorbed this speck of ours—

the free world, the dark continents,
strung together in a necklace of voice

as if a rosary among malcontents
broadcast rain for the African Service.

Liner Notes

The farther out to sea you go
the deeper is the sea's deep blue.

The liner's speed seems too slow,
and when you look there's nothing new.

Jazz club, restaurants, a Broadway show:
you've been to cities with less to do,

and overcome by muchness go
in search of a quiet just for you.

Where is it you are trying to go?
Restless heart with time to skew.

Analyze the churn of undertow,
the dragging line some fool cut through.

Imagine Hart Crane's eyes were blue.
Look: they're are staring back at you —

lanes of Masefield's galleon cargoes,
clotted weeds bound for sargassos,

voyages fancied or journeys true,
in-your-face winds always blow.

A star, a path, a current's flow.
The ink trail leads you somewhere new.

OCEANS

Get tuxed for dinner. Watch the show.
Swallow your sea but let it go.

You can't hold it; it holds you.
Think you know it, but it knows you.

It knows the shallows, that paler blue,
depth of soul where you cannot go.

Knows the caverns you deny are true.
It longs to speak in spite of you,

while certainties you claimed to know
are out there and want to drown you.

My Beautiful Father

What unfinished dreams
in your upturned palms

wait for you to wake again?
Snow falls. The grey sea calms.

Here is your faith and its pain.
I follow you on the horizon.

Drowning in Books

The summer my grandfather was dying
I read *King Lear* until it broke my heart.
I buried the old man with all his stories.

When my daughter was born I read to her
in the darkness of the neo-natal ward—
Genesis. We had to start somewhere.

Or when my family drove to the Maritimes
to watch the tidal bore reverse and waves
tear at the Cabot Trail's stone feet—

I was waiting in a room at Montale's house,
reading poetry in his library by the sea
until I looked up and was home again.

Or the day I went to return a friend's copy
of *Pilgrim's Progress* and through the dorm door
heard sounds of lovemaking for the first time;

and I went to the library, looked up Sappho,
Byron, Graves and Pushkin to make sure
that what I'd heard was true. It was.

On my honeymoon cruise, just after
lifeboat drill as the blue Caribbean opened
and its arms embraced us with a tropical night,

I checked my pocket and Matthew Arnold
was still there, avoiding his wedding night
by moaning about a Sophoclean sea.

I have a house; the basement awash in books,
and every time I descend to go reading
I am swept away by what wasn't my life.

Life can't be lived vicariously though words
are a comfort if my breath's sucked away
by a beautiful line, a fine idea, an epiphany

aimed like a torpedo through a white sea,
waking me from other people's dreams,
begging me to walk it through the world.

Just now I watch my daughter in the garden,
my wife laughing in the brilliant sunlight.
I surface, close the covers, and join them.

Home Port

Her picture on my desk so I wouldn't forget,
working late nights I'd remember my home.
The seas would change from black to red,
the executive gods were heartless bastards.

Sacrifice, courage: no matter, they wanted more,
and there's more to the world than I can tell her.
But I am home now, key sparking in the door,
the solution to a puzzle I wish I had solved

before the seas made a map of my face,
before snows of unclimbable mountains
turned longing white in my hair—
I am home now. I will make a late dinner.

I will stand by her room as she is sleeping,
listen to her breathing as if a gentle tide.
The heart begs, the life must follow.
Daughter, may you live your dreams.

Oceans

Our front door is a harbour,
porch light a sign of life;

I am bruised, your sailor,
the city sold to strife.

I've known a citizen's sufferings,
have tasted coined belief,

and all world's burnt offerings
cannot offer me relief.

Blown off, I saw the light,
our door open to the sea,

braziers glowing bright,
your shadow, Penelope,

combing out the threads—
days knotted into stories,

stories knotted in our heads;
tomorrow is for memories,

memories left for dead.
When they tempted me

with kingdoms, when they said,
You will dance to our tune, you'll see,

OCEANS

the wrack was all that's mine.
Our faces face to face

on a pillow; in outline
of your cheeks I trace

with humid, leeward breath,
the sea lanes of your salty eyes.

I sailed until I'd sailed to death,
lured by stars in godless skies.

Let's leave the stories
to someone else,

forgo the hard-won glories
for the simple love of pulse.

Life restarts itself each dawn
from a sea of tangled sheets,

failed poems Time worked on,
in a bloody maze of streets,

pursuing each possibility,
lines scribbled on a draft,

there on our heads for all to see,
the wake of a travelled craft.

Forget those wine-dark days.
I am home and you are home.

Such tears we shed for praise,
language wearing away at stone

awash in words unmeaningful,
ebb when I say your name:

yet the moth is never as beautiful
as when it embraces the flame.

NOTES

"In Sand, To a Daughter Approaching Seven." The mention of Caedmon, the first English Christian poet, is a reference to the beginning of English poetry as told by the Venerable Bede in Book IV, Chapter 24 of *A History of the Church and English People* (Historica Ecclesiastica Gentis Anglorum, c. 731). There Bede tells the miraculous story of how the touch of an angel inspired an illiterate stable-hand at the Abbey of Whitby to set the entire Bible into Old English verse.

"The Odysseus Limericks." The limerick, as a poetic form, originated in France in the 12th century as a form of "mad song."

"Bref Double by Candlelight" was written on Manitoulin Island, where there was electricity, during the big blackout of August, 2003. The bref double, according to Lewis Turco's *New Book of Forms*, "is thought to be an ancestor of the sonnet," and likely dates from the 10th or 11th century.

"Tempest." This poem in rimas dissolutas, owes a debt of gratitude to Michael Wood's very readable book, *Shakespeare*, and to Leon Rooke's delightful novel *Shakespeare's Dog*.

"Ties." A foreign hand is one of several knots that can be used to tie a neck-tie.

"Navigatio" is the Latin word most often applied to a written account of a voyage, such as the *Navigatio Brendanum* of the 11th century, which chronicles the seven-year voyage of St. Brendan from Ireland to what appears to be North America or paradise.

"Kingfishers from the Subway." The view from the subway that is mentioned in the poem is that from the Prince Edward Viaduct in Toronto (also known as the Bloor Street Viaduct) that spans the Don Valley. During the spring of 2003, a pair of kingfishers lived in the Donlands. The story of the drowned king is that of Ceyx and Alcyone, told by Ovid in *The Metamorphoses*. Ovid suggests that as a result of having been turned into kingfishers through the pity of the gods, Ceyx and Alcyone annually build their nests on the calm waters of the Mediterranean, an ornithological urban legend which has given rise to the term 'halcyon days.'

"The Lighthouse at Honfleur." This poem is based on a painting by Georges Seurat . It hangs in the National Gallery of Art in Washington, D.C. The painting depicts a beach scene with a lighthouse in the background and a small boat sailing calmly by itself. The painting is startling for its absence of any human figures in the scene.

"Royal Life-Saving Course." In Classical tragedy, the actors wore masks in order to portray their characters. These masks were known as "persona," a term that is now applied in literary critical language to the speaker of a poem.

"Blue Heaven" was the name of a small cottage my family rented at West Harwich on Cape Cod the summer I was thirteen.

"Inland." This poem is for my late father-in-law, Cecil Ross Johnston, who was a uranium miner in Elliot Lake, Ontario.

"Homeric Laughter" is an old, cliché term from the nineteenth century which suggests hearty laughter.

MEYER

The oxymoron behind the phrase suggests a kind of operatic tension; laughter in the face of inevitability and inescapable destiny. Peter D'Epiro and Mary Desmond Pinkowish in their book, *Sprezzatura: 50 Ways Italian Genius Shaped the World,* describe the origins of opera. They tell of the proceedings of the Florentine Camerata of the Quattrocento, a collection of artists who attempted new forms of art, science and discourse. Among the members of Camerata was a court composer of the Medici named Vincenzi Galilei, the father of the astronomer Galileo whose theories eventually altered the perceived structure of the solar system.

"The River-Merchant's Boys" is a traditional glose (often mis-named a glossa). The form, originally a Spanish and Portuguese poem of commentary, uses the first two lines from a "text" as the opening couplet, and repeats the same lines later in the same stanza. I am not sure what nonce forms pass for gloses in Canada— the term has been abused by various poets. In the case of this poem I have stolen the first six lines from Ezra Pound's beautiful poem, "The River-Merchant's Wife," a poem that tells the story of lovers who have grown up together in ancient China. My apologizes to Pound.

"The Rainy Season." Until the recent erection of anti-suicide barriers on the Prince Edward Viaduct in Toronto, there were coin-operated binoculars on the bridge that allowed one a close-up view of the downtown financial district. The binoculars were so effective that on clear days one could see office workers moving about on the upper floors of the bank towers almost two miles away.

"Trompe l'Oeil." The term literally means "to fool the eye." In Chatsworth House in Derbyshire, one of

England's great stately homes, there is the famous violin door— a realistic painting of a violin that is often covered with a heavy oak door. The joke was that in slamming the door, the almost three-dimensional violin would appear to be crushed, though in reality the painting was merely a one-dimensional surface.

"Parade of Lights." Each Christmas, around December 20 in the coastal beach area of St. Petersburg, Florida, the local yachtsmen decorate their ships in a variety of seasonal themes and parade them, after sunset, through the intercoastal waterways. The site of the decorated ships is both campy and memorable.

"Liner Notes." The poem of John Masefield's that I am referring to is "Cargoes," a riot of metrical variations that discusses the various types of ships through the ages that have plied the seas, each carrying a cargo reflective of the epoch. Hart Crane, the American poet, committed suicide by jumping from the back of an ocean liner.

"Drowning in Books." Matthew Arnold is said to have written his famous poem, "Dover Beach," while on his honeymoon, possibly his wedding night. The composition of the poem, one of the most beautiful downers ever composed, coincides with the creation of Canada as a nation almost to the hour on July 1, 1867.

Acknowledgements

"The Lighthouse at Honfleur" appeared previously in *Shenandoah* and in my first collection of poetry, *The Open Room* (Black Moss Press, 1989).

"Ties" and "Katie and the Bouquet of Dandelions" appeared in *Variety Crossings #5*, edited by Dae-Tong Huh and published by the Korean-Canadian Literary Forum. These poems were translated into Korean by Dae-Tong Huh.

"Going to Nantucket" and "The Odysseus Limericks" appeared in *Variety Crossings #6*, edited by Dae-Tong Huh and published by the Korean-Canadian Literary Forum. These poems were translated into Korean by Hannah Kim.

The author is grateful to Barry Callaghan, Halli Villegas, Dae-Tong Huh, Fred Addis, Terry O'Malley, Fred Fallis, Bill Gordon, Mimi Marrocco, Robert Sward, David Wevill, Priscila Uppal and Chris Doda for the ongoing feedback, opportunity and the encouragement they provided as these poems evolved. A very special thanks to Carolyn Meyer, soothsayer, sounding-board, and sibling deluxe.

And to those who stood by me through the storms, we shall sail again someday.

BIOGRAPHY

Bruce Meyer is author of 22 textbooks, poetry and fiction collections and anthologies including *The Golden Thread: A Reader's Journey Through the Great Books*, the poetry collections *The Open Room, Radio Silence, The Presence, Anywhere* and *The Spirit Bride*. With Barry Callaghan he co-edited *We Wasn't Pals: Canadian Poetry and Prose of the First World War* and *The Selected Poems of Frank Prewett*. With Jonathan Barron he co-edited the *Dictionary of Literary Biography* volume on *The New Formalists* The radio broadcasts on *The Great Books* with Michael Enright have been heard nationally and internationally, and he is a frequent panelist on TV Ontario. His poetry has won numerous prizes including the Ruth Cable Memorial Award, the E.J. Pratt Gold Medal and Prize for Poetry, and the Alta Lind Cook Award for Writing. He has been Visiting Writer at the University of Texas and the University of Southern Mississippi, is Artistic Director of the Leacock Summer Literary Festival in Orillia, Ontario, and has taught at various Canadian and American universities. He lives in Toronto and is a professor of English at the Laurentian University Program at Georgian College in Barrie and in the St. Michael's College Continuing Education Program at the University of Toronto.